Help Your Parents ®
SAVE THE PLANET

Help Your Parents®

SAVE THE

50 Simple Ways

E PLANET

to Go Green Now!

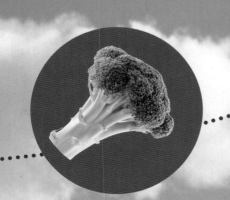

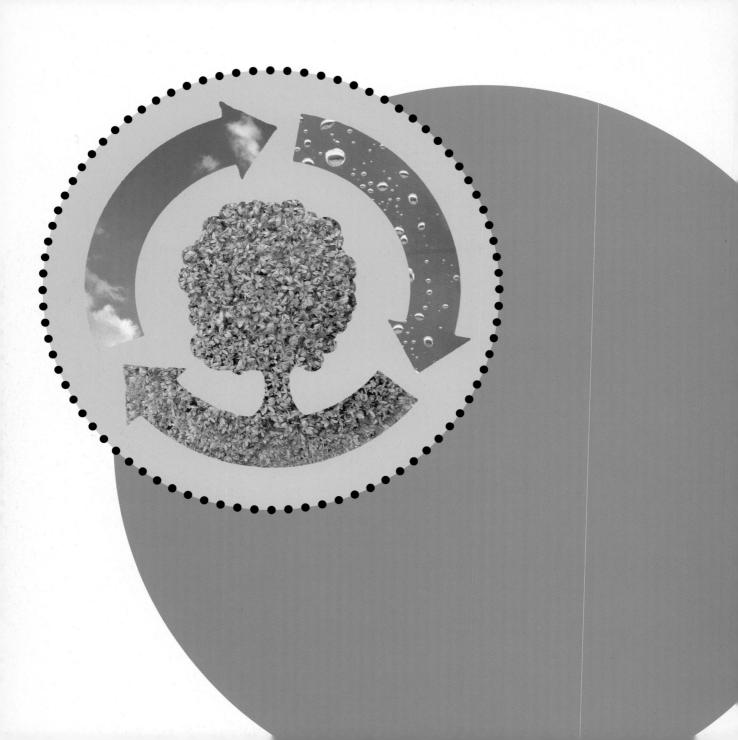

Contents

Introduction to a green lifestyle

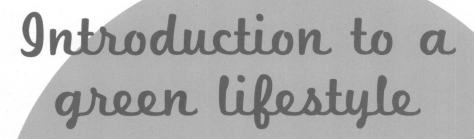

Saving the planet isn't as hard as you think – you don't even need superpowers to do it! This book contains many different ways you can help your parents, brothers, sisters, and your friends to protect the environment and make the world a cleaner, more beautiful place.

Each tip is easy to do and completely FREE! Saving the planet doesn't have to cost anything, and some of these tips can actually help save your family money.

Before you get started, try to remember a few simple things:

- First, don't worry about doing everything all at once. Take it slowly; maybe try one new idea each day or each week. Going green is about changing the way we live, and it may take time to teach your parents everything you'll learn here. The important thing is to keep trying!

- Second, going green means not always doing or buying everything you want, which may be difficult at first. Just remember that many small sacrifices and tiny changes can make a big impact on the earth – and the power to make these changes is in your hands!

- The last thing to remember is to have a good time! Sharing these ideas and tips with family and friends is part of the fun. Encouraging others to adopt a green lifestyle is rewarding for you and for the environment.

You know better. You *can* make a difference.
So what are you waiting for? Let's go save the planet!

Go green in the kitchen!

Don't worry! Going green in the kitchen doesn't mean painting the walls! It means doing things that help save the planet.

All these tips are simple and easy to do. But that doesn't mean that they aren't important – if everyone followed these suggestions, the earth would be a much healthier and greener planet. So let's get started making the world a better, more beautiful place!

Switch to cloth napkins

Napkins are made of paper, which comes from trees. So, the fewer napkins we use, the fewer trees we need to cut down.

Ask if you can help choose cloth napkins that your family can wash with the laundry and reuse instead of using paper napkins that get thrown away. See how simple this is?

Save the paper plates and cups for picnics!

When you're at home, use regular cups and plates, not paper ones. It's such an easy thing to do and it helps save trees and cut down on the amount of garbage that ends up in landfills.

A landfill is another name for a garbage dump that gets covered over with soil. [See the tip on page 38 about ways you can make your picnic even greener!]

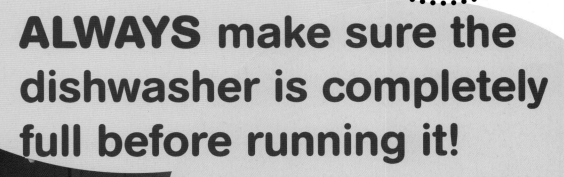

ALWAYS make sure the dishwasher is completely full before running it!

Every time you use your dishwasher it uses water, and energy to heat the water.

To make sure you're not being wasteful, always be sure your family fills the dishwasher completely before running it!

Eat what you buy – don't let food go to waste!

Did you know that Americans waste about 14% of all the food they purchase? That's like dumping one drawer of food from your refrigerator into the garbage every week!

When you go to the grocery store with your parents, ask them to consider how much food your family actually needs, and help choose items everyone intends to eat so that they won't go to waste. And remember: Eating leftovers is good for you and good for the planet!

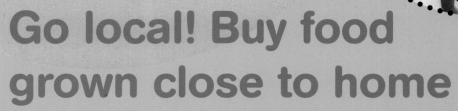

Go local! Buy food grown close to home

Does your town have a farmer's market or farm stands nearby? If so, that's a great place to buy fresh food! Did you know that some of the fruits and vegetables in many big supermarkets come from far away places across the country or even from other countries? It requires a lot of fuel, energy, and packaging to transport these food items so far from where they're grown.

Locally grown food is fresher. It's better for you and better for the environment! Read fruit and vegetable stickers and packing crates at the store to learn how close to home your food was grown.

ALWAYS bring your own bag to the store!

Each year, the world uses somewhere between 500 billion and 1 trillion (1,000,000,000,000) plastic bags! That's a lot of zeros! Many of these end up in landfills where it can take hundreds of years before they break down and become a part of the earth.

Both paper and plastic bags have a disadvantage: They create more garbage! By asking your parents to bring reusable canvas bags to the store, you are doing the earth a huge favor!

OATMEAL CONTAINER MARACAS
All you need is:
- One or two empty cylindrical oatmeal containers with plastic lids
- Dry beans, dry peas, uncooked rice, or a combination
- Supplies for decorating, such as markers, paint, and stickers

Throw a generous handful of dry beans into the oatmeal container and snap the lid on tight.

Decorate your maracas any way you like.

Shake! Shake! Shake!

No Beans? No Problem!

You can tape two oatmeal canisters (with lids on) together to make a great set of bongos!

5

Cook meals with your parents!

You can help save the planet just by cooking with your parents! Not only is cooking at home better for your health, it's better for the earth, too.

So next time Mom or Dad asks you what you want for dinner, don't suggest going out to eat or getting take-out. Remember, food "to-go" means more packaging and garbage. Instead, suggest something you can cook together at home!

Buy fresh food instead of frozen food!

Many types of frozen foods can be prepared from fresh ingredients. For instance, instead of buying frozen pizza, ask your parents if you can help them make pizza from scratch.

Not only is it healthier, it helps cut down on the packaging and **energy** used for frozen pizzas. Besides, learning to make dough is much more fun than opening a box. Can you think of other types of frozen foods that you can make fresh?

Tap water is just as good as bottled water!

In fact, it's better. It's much better for the environment and cheaper than bottled water. That's because tap water comes straight from your kitchen faucet – no bottle; no garbage!

So ask your parents to stop buying bottled water and drink tap water instead!

BOTTLED WATER IS JUST PLAIN WASTEFUL!

Bottles of water are among the most common beverages sold. Sadly, the plastic bottles that the water comes in are often not recycled. Some estimates report up to 52 billion plastic water bottles per year are sent to landfills instead of being recycled! We are also creating tons and tons of unnecessary garbage that takes up space in our landfills.

And it isn't just a garbage problem: Because plastic is made from crude oil, when we don't recycle it, we are wasting oil!

And that means wasting a ton of natural resources.

The best way to help cut down on all this waste is simple: Don't drink bottled water! If you do end up having a bottle every once in a while, just make sure to recycle it.

Plant a garden!

Gardens are great for the planet and a lot of fun, too! The more food your family can grow at home, the less they will need to buy at the store. Ask your parents if they'll help you start a garden in your backyard.

Even a small garden is good for the environment. **If you don't have space for a garden, see Page 11 for ideas on how to have an indoor garden!**

1. FIND A GOOD SPOT FOR YOUR GARDEN

You need a spot that gets lots of sunlight and is easy to get water to. If part of your garden doesn't get much sunlight, that's okay – there are plenty of plants that grow well in the shade, such as lettuce and spinach.

2. CHECK THE SOIL

Once you find a good spot for your garden, you need to make sure the soil isn't too hard or too dry. Also check to see if water pools on the surface (not so good) or soaks into the ground (better). Finally, condition your soil by adding some compost. **Flip to page 12 for instructions on making your own compost.**

3. PLAN YOUR GARDEN

Ask you parents to take you to a gardening store or help you look online to find information on what will grow best where you live. Choose fruits or vegetables that you like to eat so that you can make the most of your garden. **You can grow a salad with greens and a few tomato plants!** Once you have a good idea of what will work best in your garden, ask your famiy to help you do the digging and planting.

4. WATCH YOUR GARDEN GROW!

This is the really fun part! Each day you can check on your garden and see how things are coming along. But remember, the work isn't done once everything is planted! You still must water and care for your garden. **Most gardens need about an inch of rain a week.** So if you live in a dry area, or it hasn't rained lately, you'll have to water your garden.

5. HARVEST TIME!

If everything goes well, all your hard work will have paid off and you'll be able to harvest your garden by the end of summer! Imagine eating mashed potatoes that you've grown, boiled, and smashed yourself. Yummy!

Make a rain gauge and collect rainwater for your garden!

This is a great way to figure out how often you need to water your garden. It is also a great way to collect water for your garden. All you need is a large bucket and a ruler.

1. Tape the ruler inside the bucket or container with some strong duct tape. Make sure that the bottom of the ruler is flush with the bottom of the container.

2. Now, find a place to leave your rain gauge. It's best if you leave it close to your garden. Every time it rains, check the gauge by seeing how high the water is on the ruler. Record the amount in a notebook so that you can keep track of how much water your garden is getting.

3. Remember that your garden needs about an inch of water each week! Now you have an idea of how much water your garden gets from rain, and how much you need to water it.

4. To collect rainwater, find several large containers (like empty buckets). Place them in areas where they will collect the most rainwater, like below the edge of your house's roof, where water will run off and fall into the container. Every time you need to water your garden, use this water instead of water from a hose. It might be a little more work, but it helps save water!

Garden indoors!

Just because you don't have space outside for a garden doesn't mean you can't have one inside!

1. Save containers that you might otherwise recycle, like yogurt cups and coffee cans. Wash them out, and ask your parents to help you poke holes in the bottom.

2. Fill the containers with soil and place them on a tray (so the water that drains out doesn't make a mess). Find a window that gets a lot of sunlight and place your tray near it so that the containers get plenty of light.

3. Ask your parents to help you find different herb plants or seeds that will grow well, such as basil, cilantro, chives, parsley, and sage.

4. Water your herbs when the soil feels dry to the touch.

5. When your plants are at least a foot high and very leafy, they are ready for picking. Use them when your family cooks recipes that call for fresh herbs!

Start a compost pile!

A compost pile is a great way of disposing of organic materials that your family might otherwise throw away, such as orange peels, coffee grounds, eggshells, leaves, and grass clippings.

 Not only does composting cut down on how much garbage ends up in landfills, but compost can be used to help fertilize and nourish your garden, helping the environment at the same time!

PICK A SPOT

Your compost pile should be easily accessible to your garden, but not in the middle of your yard (they can be a little stinky). It's best if the pile gets some sunlight and some rain, but not too much of either. **You don't need too large of an area for your compost pile – it can be as small as 3 feet by 3 feet.** Ask your parents to contain the pile by putting a chicken wire fence around the area.

LAYERS, LAYERS, LAYERS

The key to a good compost pile is layering the different types of materials you put in it. The first layer should be a combination of food scraps (everything except meat) added to grass clippings and leaves. It should be about a foot thick. The next layer should be some fertilizer that you use in your garden (this will help speed up the process). That layer can be just an inch or two thick. The final layer should be soil from your backyard and should also be just an inch or two.

TURN, TURN, TURN

For your compost pile to work, you'll have to ask your parents to turn it every week or so. Use a shovel to move the materials on the bottom to the top. This helps the stinky stuff decompose faster. You can also continue to add new layers of material to your pile.

USE YOUR "GARDENER'S GOLD"

Compost is called "Gardener's Gold" because it helps boost the nutrients in the soil in your garden so that your plants and vegetables can grow really well! When your compost is ready (usually three to four months after starting your pile) work with your parents to help mix it in with the soil in your garden!

13

Use less and save more around the house!

Much of the time helping to save the planet is as easy as using less and saving more. But sometimes it takes dedication and a real effort to cut down on things you enjoy. Some changes may be hard at first.

But every time you make the effort, you are helping to make the planet a more beautiful and healthy place to live.

Take shorter showers!

Did you know that the average person uses 100 gallons of water each day and that the average five minute shower uses 15 – 25 gallons of water? That's enough to fill 100 big milk jugs a each day! Try to stay in the shower only as long as it takes to soap up and rinse off – anything more is a real waste.

Encourage everyone in your family to take shorter showers and you'll be doing the planet a favor!

Make your toilet greener!

Did you know that every time you flush the toilet, between two and seven gallons of water are used just to push the water through the pipes?

A great way to help lessen the amount of water your toilet uses is by adding "float boosters" to the toilet tank.

First you need two 16-ounce plastic bottles with screw-on lids. Put an inch or two of sand in the bottom of the bottles, fill them with water, then screw their caps on. Ask your parents to help you place them inside the toilet tank, away from any of the flushing parts. This will lower the amount of water your toilet uses for each flush.

SOME FACTS ABOUT WATER

Water is one of the earth's most precious resources. Even though it is the most common substance found on the planet and covers 80% of the earth's surface, only 1% of it is drinkable! That's because most of it is too salty to drink.

Here are some other cool facts about water:

🌍 Water is the only substance found on earth in three different forms (liquid, solid, and gas)!

🌍 **One gallon of water weighs more than seven pounds!**

🌍 When it rains just one inch, 27,000 gallons of water fall per acre!

Bundle up!

Whenever you're cold at home, just put on a sweater or sweatshirt! Heating a home requires a lot of **energy**. Turning the **thermostat** up even a few degrees means your family will be using more **fuel** oil.

If it's a little chilly inside, encourage your family to dress a little warmer instead of adjusting the heat.

Turn off the air conditioner and use a fan

Sometimes the summer heat can be downright miserable and you need to use an air conditioner to stay cool. But most of the time, a fan works just as well – without using as much **energy**!

Encourage your family to use fans instead of the air conditioner. Both the tips on this page will save your parents money on their **utility bill** and help conserve **energy**!

ALWAYS turn off lights when you leave a room!

Remind your family members to always turn out the lights when they leave a room. After all, if no one is in a room, why do the lights need to be on?

It might take everyone a little while to get in the habit of turning the lights out when they leave a room, but once they do, your family will be saving a lot of **energy**!

17

Wash clothes in cold – not hot – water

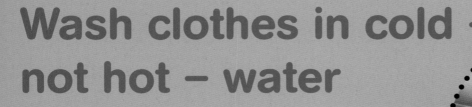

Help your parents do the laundry and suggest that they use cold water instead of hot. Cold water can wash clothes just as well as hot, but it doesn't require **energy** to be heated!

Air-dry your clothes

Instead of using a dryer to dry your clothes, air-dry them instead. If you have some room in your backyard or basement, you could install a clothesline or use a drying rack to hang clothes. You save money and **energy** by not using a dryer!

AaaaChoo! Dust your lightbulbs

Did you know that dusty lightbulbs use more **energy** than clean ones? It sounds crazy, but it's true! It won't take very much time at all to regularly check and clean the lightbulbs in your home – what a bright idea!

Curtains for cooling and warmth

Curtains aren't just for decoration! They are a great way to help control the temperature of your family's home. At night in the winter, have your parents shut them to keep the heat in and the cold out. During the day in the winter, keeping the curtains open will help let in the warmth from the sun.

In the summer, it's the opposite: Keep the curtains closed during the day to keep the heat out and open at night to let the coolness in!

Turn off the holiday lights!

Holiday lights are festive and fun, but they also use electricity. That doesn't mean you shouldn't use them, it just means that you should be sure to turn them off when you go to bed at night.

Get creative with your wrapping!

Giving and getting presents can be a ton of fun, especially if you know you aren't hurting the environment!

The next time you have a present to give, try to find a way to wrap it with recycled paper. You could use the comics section of the newspaper, or make a picture collage from old magazines. You can also use paper bags to design your own wrapping paper with stickers, stamps, and markers.

When you receive a gift, try to unwrap it as carefully as possible so that you can save and reuse the wrapping paper.

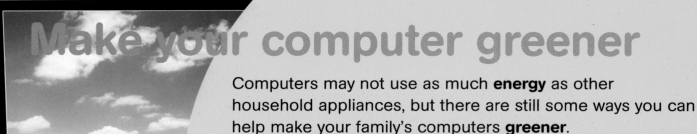

Make your computer greener

Computers may not use as much **energy** as other household appliances, but there are still some ways you can help make your family's computers **greener**.

The first thing you can ask your parents to do is plug the computer into a "smart strip." This will help reduce the power your computer uses when it's sitting idle. Another thing you can do is adjust the brightness of your monitors.

While you don't want to make them too dim so that it's hard on your eyes, if you turn the brightness down a little you'll help save **energy**.

ALWAYS turn off your computer when you aren't using it!

A lot of us leave our computers on all the time, even when we aren't using them. That doesn't mean you need to shut off your computer if you're just taking a little break. But if you're going to bed, or leaving the house for the day, there is no reason your computer needs to be on.

Even if it's "sleeping," it is still using and wasting **energy**.

POWER

The Three R's: Reduce! Reuse! Recycle!

FOLLOWING THE THREE R'S IS A GRRREAT WAY TO HELP SAVE THE PLANET

The three R's stand for Reduce, Reuse, and Recycle. By getting your family to follow them, you can help reduce the amount of waste your family produces by reusing some items and recycling others!

So far, a lot of the things we've already talked about involve the three R's. In the following pages, we will look at what each R really means and give you some more examples of things you can do to help the environment.

But first, let's talk about why this is important.

Each day, the average American can create more than 4 pounds of trash! This might sound impossible, but it's actually pretty easy to accumulate.

Most of this trash is packaging, which is the wrapping that products come in. Most of this packaging never gets recycled. That means it ends up in landfills. Why is that bad? Because eventually we'll run out of places to put all our trash!

Following the three R's is one way to help make sure that this never happens.

ALWAYS snip six-pack rings!

When six-pack rings get thrown away, they can hurt animals that may get stuck in the holes or that accidentally eat the rings.

Cut apart each circle before you throw the six-pack rings away. That way, animals can't get trapped in them!

Reduce!

This is the first R and maybe the easiest one, too! That's because you don't actually have to do anything except **use less stuff**. That's it!

Did you know that if everyone on the planet used as much stuff as we do in the United States, the world would have to be three to five times bigger to hold all of us?

So next time you are at the store thinking of buying something, make sure you really, really need it.

Precycle

The best way to reduce how much stuff you throw away is by not bringing it into your home in the first place!

Ask your parents to try to buy products with packaging that can be easily recycled.

Source Reduction

Source reduction is when the people who make products try to use less packaging around their products. Your family can't really practice source reduction, but you **can** choose to buy products that weren't packaged wastefully. Here are two ways you can help with source reduction:

1. Ask your parents **not** to buy single-serve containers. For instance, your parents can buy juice in large, recyclable jugs and pour servings into cups. This is much less wasteful than buying a bunch of juice boxes!

2. Ask your parents to buy things in bulk. Buying in bulk is when you buy a large quantity of something that isn't divided into individual packages. This helps cut down on wasteful packaging. Remember, your parents should only buy things in bulk that won't go to waste!

   With just a little bit of effort to reduce the amount of garbage you create, you can help save the planet!

Reuse!

Have you ever heard the expression, "One man's trash is another man's treasure"? Well, that's exactly what the second R is all about: finding ways to reuse items you might otherwise throw away.

- **Just because something is "disposable" doesn't mean you have to throw it in the trash after using it once.** For example, plastic utensils, plastic cups, and plastic containers can all be washed and reused again and again!
- Use yogurt containers with lids and egg cartons to store craft supplies such as beads, string, shells, and extra glue and paint.
- When you need something new, like a bicycle or bed or desk, ask your parents if you can try to find the item at a yard sale or in a thrift store. Getting brand-new things can be nice, but it's also wasteful! Especially if you can find the same item that is just slightly used. **Be creative in thinking up new uses for old toys, containers, and household objects.**
- Learn to fix things! Just because the kitchen table has a wobbly leg doesn't mean you need to get a whole new table. Ask your parents if you can help them fix things around the house instead of replacing them. **You'll be amazed at what a little effort can do to make something seem almost new again!**

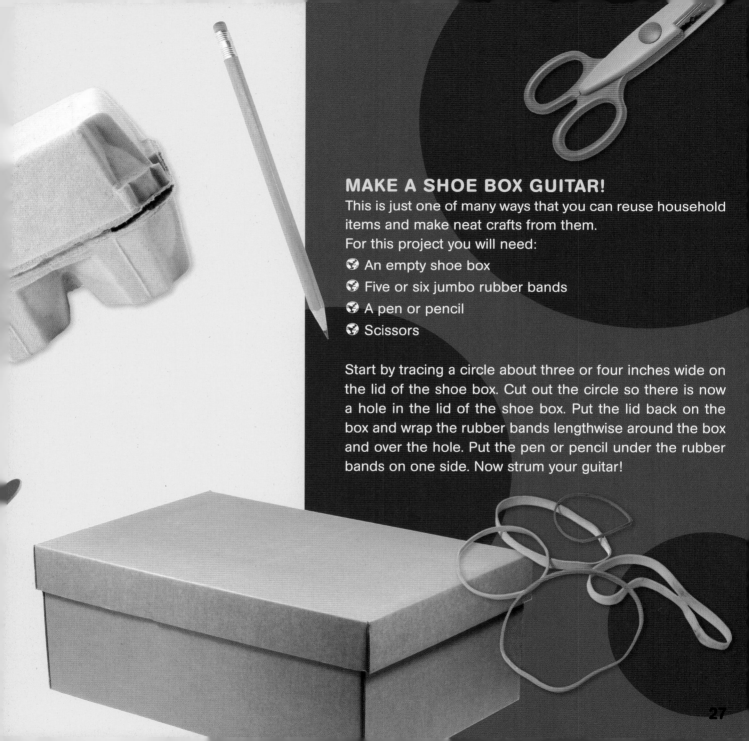

MAKE A SHOE BOX GUITAR!

This is just one of many ways that you can reuse household items and make neat crafts from them.

For this project you will need:

- An empty shoe box
- Five or six jumbo rubber bands
- A pen or pencil
- Scissors

Start by tracing a circle about three or four inches wide on the lid of the shoe box. Cut out the circle so there is now a hole in the lid of the shoe box. Put the lid back on the box and wrap the rubber bands lengthwise around the box and over the hole. Put the pen or pencil under the rubber bands on one side. Now strum your guitar!

Recycle!

No matter how much reducing and reusing we do, we'll probably always have some garbage. That's where the third R, Recycling, comes in!

What can be recycled?

These days, many different things can be recycled! The trick is figuring out where they need to go and when.

Most cities in the United States have recycling programs for common items such as plastics, paper and cardboard, glass, and aluminum. There are other items that should always be recycled, but are a little trickier, such as batteries, electronics, different metals, paints and chemicals, and appliances. See pages 44-45 to learn more about what the recycling symbols on different products mean.

Take Action!

- Start a glue recycling program at your school. Visit www.elmersglue.com for details.
- Crocs shoes can be recycled into new Crocs. Visit www.SolesUnited.com for information, or simply mail your used crocs to Crocs Recycling West, 3375 Enterprise Avenue, Bloomington, CA 92316.
- Recycle your old crayons by sending them to the National Crayon Recycle program. Go to www.crazycrayons.com for details.

Recycle with your family!

Once you know what can be recycled and where, help your family get in the habit of sorting things that are recyclable from things that are not. Be sure your parents set up recycling bins next to your main garbage can. Clearly label each bin so that everyone knows what goes where.

If your city picks up the recycling like they do garbage, keep a schedule next to the bins so you know when to take them out for pickup. Otherwise, when the bins get full, have your parents help you take them to the local recycling center.

Now that you know the three R's, it's time to put them to use!

NEVER, EVER LITTER!

Littering is one of the absolute worst things you can do to the environment. **All trash should always be thrown away in a garbage can or put in a recycling bin if it's recyclable.** So don't be a litterbug and never, ever throw trash on the ground!

If you have some trash and can't find a garbage can, put it in your pocket or backpack until you can find one. If you see a friend or family member litter, tell them how bad it is for the environment and ask them to pick it up.

When someone litters, the trash can end up in the oceans, rivers, and forests. Not only is litter ugly and dirty, it is dangerous for animals and illegal in most states.

ALWAYS save and reuse your school supplies!

At the beginning of each school year you probably get a list of supplies you'll need from your teacher. A lot of these items are the same types of things year after year — notebooks, pencils, paper, markers, and folders.

At the end of each school year, put all you school supplies that you can still use in a drawer for safe keeping.

Then, have a fun summer! When the next year begins, check the drawer before buying new supplies. This is a great way to reduce and reuse.

Use your bike and use your feet!

As you probably know, driving a car uses a lot of fuel. A great way to save money for your family and help the environment is to ride your bike and to walk more!

Whenever your family needs to go somewhere nearby, ask you parents if you can ride bikes or walk there. Be a team leader to get your family moving!

Bike riding and walking are both good exercise, and neither of them causes any pollution or use any **natural resources**! They're also great ways to spend time with your family!

Map out your errands!

Make a game out of running errands by mapping out the shortest route.

Instead of piling into the car, design a bike or walking route that passes all the stops your family needs to make. It may not be quicker, but it could be a lot more fun!

Help organize a carpool!

A carpool is a really fun and simple way to help your parents and your friends' parents use less gas by having them take turns driving you and your friends places.

Think about it: If you have five friends and you all go to the same school, why should your parents take you in five different cars for sports practices and other activities?

Less cars=Less pollution.

Green fashions!

Another area where you can go **green** is with your wardrobe! Instead of buying new clothes each school year, get together with friends to trade different items of clothing. Start a trend of hand-me-down fashions from your older brothers and sisters.

And if you want to be really creative, you can also learn to knit, crochet, and sew your own clothes for one-of-a-kind fashions.

Unplug and Save!

Anything that uses electricity – from radios to video games to phone chargers – should be unplugged when not in use.

Everything that is plugged in (whether on or off) uses and wastes electricity.

ALWAYS recycle your phone book!

Every few months your family probably gets a new phone book, which means you need to get rid of the old one. Make sure you recycle it!

For every 500 phone books that are recycled, 17 – 31 trees, and enough electricity to power a home for six months, are saved!

Be creative with cartons!

BIRDHOUSE

- Cut a hole in the side of a carton about 1/2 inch diameter for the birds to get in and out of.
- Poke drainage holes in the bottom of the carton.
- Poke another hole through the top of the carton, and thread with string, yarn, or twine to hang from a tree.

FLOWER POT

- Cut off the top of a carton to make your "pot" the size you want.
- Fill with soil to about two inches from the top.
- Add plants or seeds, water, and GROW!

PLANT PROTECTORS
☻ Cut off both ends of the carton to form a square "tube."
☻ Place over seedlings in your garden to protect them until the plants are stronger and sturdier.

CARTON BOWLING
☻ Save 10 quart-size cartons.
☻ Fill each with four inches of sand.
☻ Reseal the tops of all the cartons with either duct tape or a stapler and staples.
☻ Set 'em up and bowl!

37

Clean up your local park!

Do you like having picnics and playing in the park? Well, how about having some fun and doing something good for the environment, too!

Organizing a clean-up day at your local park can be a really fun way to meet new friends and make sure your park is a clean and safe place to play at.

GET THE WORD OUT!
1. Once you pick a date and time to have your clean-up day, you need to let all your friends and neighbors know! **You can even ask your teacher to make this a class project.**

ORGANIZE
2. You'll need plenty of trash bags for all the garbage you pick up. It's best if you have different colored bags to separate trash from things that can be recycled, such as cans and paper.

BE SAFE
3. This is really important. There can be a lot of sharp or dangerous pieces of trash. If you don't know what something is, don't pick it up. Ask a parent to help you! It would also be a good idea if everyone had latex gloves to wear so their hands don't get dirty.

HAVE FUN!
4. Make sure the clean-up day is fun. You can have rewards for whoever collects the most garbage. Or you can have races to see who cleans up an area the quickest. You might want to bring some games and activities to play once all the work is done!

At the end of a clean-up day, the park will look much better and you'll know that it's because of you and your friends.

ALWAYS dispose of batteries properly

Batteries contain a lot of dangerous chemicals and cannot be thrown away with regular trash. And they cannot be recycled along with glass, plastic, and paper.

Ask your parents or teachers to help you find where batteries can be recycled in your town by looking online or in the phone book. Always save your old batteries in a safe spot until they can be recycled properly.

Keep that balloon close!

Sometimes it can be fun to let go of a helium-filled balloon and watch it float off in the sky.

But it's bad for the environment! Eventually that balloon falls back to earth and becomes litter. Deflated balloons are especially bad because animals can accidentally choke on them and even die.

So the next time you have a floating balloon, make sure not to let it go – better yet: Tie it safely to something stable.

Do you really need to print that?

One of the really awesome things about email is that it is completely **green**, meaning that it doesn't use any **natural resources**. The amount of paper saved because of email is tremendous.

Of course, if you print an email, it's no longer **green**. So unless you really, really have to print them, read your emails on the computer screen!

Read it online!

Anything you can read online saves the trees it would normally take to print it on paper. Newspapers, catalogs, yellow-page listings, maps with directions, and weather and news updates can all be found and read online.

Make sure your family looks online first!

Stop the junk mail!

Does your family get a ton of **junk mail**? Did you know that nearly 1 trillion pieces of **junk mail** are mailed each year? That's a huge waste of paper!

There is a way to reduce the amount of unwanted paper in you mailbox. All you need to do is visit the Direct Marketing Association's mail preference website and request that your family's name be removed from mailing lists.

Here's the link: https://www.dmachoice.org/MPS/proto1.php

Make the **junk mail** stop and you'll be going **green** with less paper waste at your house.

THE TRUTH ABOUT PAPER

Did you know that it's estimated that the average American uses 700 pounds of paper a year? That's a ton of paper! Well actually, it's closer to half a ton, but you get the point.

Paper comes from trees, and trees are incredibly important to the health of our planet. You see, trees absorb carbon, which is one of the chemicals that causes global warming. So the more trees we cut down, the less carbon they can absorb, and the hotter our planet will get.

Right now, we are using trees faster than we can replace them. And if we keep it up, someday there won't be any trees at all!

It's really, really important to use as little paper as possible, and to always recycle the paper we do use.

What's that symbol mean? A guide to the different recycling symbols

 This is the universal recycling symbol. Products marked with this symbol can and should be recycled.

 Packages or containers stamped with this symbol were made from at least some recycled materials.

 Soft drink and water bottles can usually can be recycled through your town's curbside recycling program. This plastic is recycled into polar fleece, furniture, and carpet.

 Milk jugs, shampoo bottles, and some trash and shopping bags can be easily recycled and turned into pens, floor tiles, drainage pipes, and fencing.

PVC House siding, windows, piping, and some bottles are not usually recyclable. Check with your local recycling program before including these items with your curbside recycling.

 LDPE Squeezable bottles, furniture, and carpet. Check with your local recycling program before including these with your curbside recycling.

 PP Caps, straws, and medicine bottles all contain this type of plastic. Usually recycled into battery cables, ice scrapers, and rakes.

 PS Egg cartons and CD cases are both made of this type of plastic. It can usually be recycled at your curbside and turned into insulation, rulers, and carry-out containers.

 OTHER Three- and five-gallon water containers, sunglasses, iPod and computer cases, and DVDs all use this type of plastic. Check with your local recycling program before including these plastics with your curbside recycling.

Spread the word!

Here is one of the most important tips in the whole book: Tell everyone you know how important it is that we start treating the planet better! One person can do a lot of damage by being wasteful, so it's important that everyone try their best to reduce, reuse, and recycle.

You can spread the word about going **green** in many different ways. Here are a few:

Write emails!

Is your school being wasteful by serving lunch on disposable plates? Write a letter to the principal and the school board about why they should have reusable plates.

Does your town have enough recycling bins next to trash cans? Write a letter to the city council or the local newspaper telling them why recycling is important. Big changes in this world have been the result of people who write letters – and you can be one of those people!

46

Tell your friends and family

Let the people you love know that you love the environment, too. When you are committed to "living **green**," you can lead by example and by politely letting others know that you care enough not to litter or waste **energy** and resources.

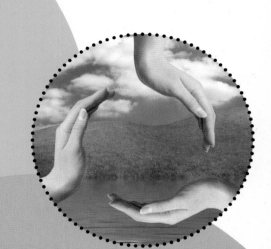

Volunteer

Volunteering is a great way to meet other people who want to help save the planet. Joining together with environmental groups for kids is a cool way to make friends and find out new ways to spread the word about helping the planet.

Just one person can't save the earth. But one person can make a difference. Working together, we can make this planet healthy again. So spread the word and help your parents save the planet!

Glossary

BREAKDOWN is when a material or substance decomposes, rots, or "breaks" into smaller parts or its original form.

COMPOST is a mixture of decaying organic material, such as kitchen scraps and leaves, that can be used to fertilize soil.

CRUDE OIL is Oil that comes out of the ground in its raw state and hasn't been turned into gasoline or plastic yet is called crude oil.

DECOMPOSE is just a fancy way to say "rot." When something decomposes, it returns to its simpler elements.

ENERGY is any source of power, such as fuel, electricity, or solar radiation, that can be used to power things.

ENVIRONMENTALLY FRIENDLY means doing things that are good for the planet. So, for instance, following the tips in this book is being environmentally friendly.

FERTILIZER is a material or mixture of substances that help make soil more fertile so plants can grow better.

FUEL is a substance that is used to provide energy. Gasoline, kerosene, oil, and coal are all examples of different types of fuel.

GREEN is the color that symbolizes environmentally friendly products and behaviors. So when you "go green" you are doing the right thing for the environment.

JUNK MAIL is advertisements and catalogs that you haven't requested that are sent to you by companies trying to sell their products.

NATURAL RESOURCES are resources such as oil, wind, water, trees, soil, solar power, and minerals that occur naturally on planet earth.

ORGANIC means things that are grown or made naturally, without using chemicals, hormones, or drugs. Compost is an example of an organic fertilizer because it is made using only natural substances such as food scraps and leaves. Plants and food grown using only organic fertilizer are also considered organic.

SMART STRIP is a type of plug that helps conserve energy but cutting off electricity to an appliance when it's not in use. A smart strip looks like a long block of electrical outlets that can be used to plug in many appliances at once.

THERMOSTAT is a device that controls how hot or cold your house is by regulating how much heat or air conditioning is used.

UTILITY BILL is the bill your parents get each month for all the electricity, gas, and sometimes water, your household has used during the previous month. It indicates the amount of energy your family has used and the amount of money you'll need to pay.

WASTE is anything that is not used and thrown away. It is also another word for garbage.

Index

All photographs Shutterstock

Text by Gregory Rutty

Special Thanks to:
Becky Terhune, Susan Schultz, Cheryl Weisman, and Paula Manzanero

ISBN: 978-1-60214-085-1

Play Bac Publishing USA, Inc.
225 Varick Street
New York, NY 10014
www.playbac.com

Printed in China

Distributed by Black Dog & Leventhal Publishers, Inc.
151 West 19th Street
New York, NY 10011

First Printing 2009